Tantric Lesbian Sex

The Ultimate Step by Step Guide for Women to Discover Tantric Sex Positions, Tips, Ideas, and Secrets

FLORENCE BLUE

ISBN: 979-8-6892-3183-9

CONTENTS

INTRODUCTION

First of all, you have made a brilliant decision to purchase this book. Sex is an essential aspect of life. It is as necessary for physical wellbeing as it is for mental wellbeing. We live in impossibly busy times. We have become so accustomed to our hectic schedules that even 24 hours seem insufficient. The balance between work and social life is a delicate one. The struggle to maintain balance often leads people to suppress or completely ignore their sex lives. There is an alarmingly high rate of couples who have little to no sex today despite the physical and psychological benefits to a healthy relationship.

Reigniting the sexual spark in your relationship can take you on different paths. Still, one of the most successful ways is a technique called tantra. This technique has helped millions of people better communicate with their partners and ensure they attain the highest level of pleasure, and not just physically.

Tantric sex is an activity that provides emotionally and sexually satisfying experiences that make you feel connected or soul-linked to your partner.

This book is here to assist you and your beautiful woman on your journey to the ultimate sexual experience. Your sex life will be completely transformed through the knowledge of tantra. You and your partner are assured emotional, sexual, and spiritual fulfillment. This does not, in any way, mean that you haven't satisfied your partner before now. However, this is going to take it up several notches.

When you tap into the natural energy stored in your body and your partner's, you will be able to bask in orgasms like you never have. As a couple, you will discover new ways to experience physical pleasure together while performing the most basic things like gentle touches, synchronized breathing, cuddling, etc.

People find themselves trying their hands at tantric sex for various reasons. They might be looking for ways to bring back the spark or even rev up the heat. Others might just be curious about the technique. Either way, everyone who has tried tantra has this shared experience: Their perspective of sex never remains the same. I'm sure you'll find the same goes for you, as you begin this journey to Nirvana. I guarantee it's like nothing you've ever experienced before.
If you're feeling skeptical, just this once, let yourself go. You have nothing to lose and everything to gain.

1 TANTRIC SEX

Before we get to the fun part (the sex positions and all that good stuff), it is vital to understand the concept of tantric sex. Tantra goes back many years to ancient India. Several of India's holy men and saints did all sorts of rituals and meditations. Tantra's practice is believed to have existed since the 5th century AD and was seen as a means to enable an individual to grasp divine consciousness and control their conscience.

This technique is believed to have been in existence since the 5th century AD, and it was perceived as a method that would help individuals harness divine consciousness and develop their conscience. This concept traveled across the globe and resulted in the modern-day usage of the term "tantra," assuming a new meaning altogether.

The term tantra is popularly associated with the practice of Tantric sex. This involves engaging in a sexual act with the intent of garnering divine consciousness together. To put it simply, tantric sex is a practice that leads you to sexual Nirvana.

Tantric sex is comprised of three critical aspects: Tantric positions, tantric exercises, and tantric communication.

Tantric positions are various positions that will enable you and your partner to draw closer to each other sexually.

Tantric communication is the process that work to merge you and your partner mentally and emotionally.

Tantric exercises (like breathing techniques) are activities to ensure that you and your partner are ready to reap the most out of the tantric experience.

Tantric sex takes you both a step closer to the freedom of your mind, soul, and body through the practices I mentioned above. Any meditative practice requires a calm mind, and that applies to tantric sex. So, you must be open to having a mind that's relaxed and at ease. Tantra's teachings ensure that couples pay attention and maintain an awareness of their actions while participating in sexual activities-something sorely lacking in regular sex.

Mindfulness of your actions will lead you to act with a feeling of respect and reverence for your partner. It involves honoring your partner's body as well as your own. The main objective of tantric sex is to foster total relaxation of body and mind. This physical and mental freedom will then result in you being able to express yourself with unrestrained ease that will strengthen and intensify the bond between you and your woman. It will bring to life the kind of emotion that will bind your souls.

As I mentioned before, a calm and quiet mind is crucial for engaging in tantric sex. Without this inner peace, you will not be able to be an observer and participant as well. This means that you are required to be present enough to make love to her and observe your actions and your partner's actions and responses.

Once you begin to pay attention to the things that you do, you become a witness. Being a witness helps you let go of any concerns that you may have at the moment. You're not distracted by worries about whether you're doing it right or your partner's thoughts about what you're doing. All that anxiety will need to float away because worrying is bad for business in tantra.

In summary, Tantric sex can be all or any of the following:
1. Practices that direct you and your partner's energies towards openness which dissolve the barriers you harbor inside and between yourself.
2. Practices that bring about a balance between the masculine and feminine energies within you both.
3. Practices that bind you to another person and the universe through a spiritual, sexual experience.
4. Practices that celebrate sexual union as an appreciation for

2

creation itself.

5. Practices that free the soul to the opportunity of experiencing bliss at its peak.

2 BREATHING

When you breathe properly, you supply the needed oxygen to all parts of your body and ease your emotions. This simple activity can lead to ecstasy and even climax. The way you breathe is the key to more prolonged and intense sexual and orgasmic experiences. It sounds a little absurd, doesn't it? I mean, breathing is easy, we've been doing it since we came into this world, right? Check your breath right now. I can bet it is shallow and barely inflating your chest! That is the problem. We don't breathe as deeply and as much as we should, and this isn't healthy.

Let's look at three basic breathing techniques that you can practice right now for better breathing:

• The life source: Observe your body and pinpoint precisely where you're breathing. Your chest, stomach, or throat? Make an effort to ensure it comes from deep within you, and with every inhale, use your hand to pinpoint how deeply you took it before exhaling. Breathe in as deeply as you can go, making sure you reach as low as your genitals. That is how you get that sexual energy revved up.

• The Eagle pose: This is perfect for when you're sitting down. Crunch inwards like a ball and exhale as you do so. Rest both hands on the back of your head as this will bring your elbows closer to your body. Do you feel that stretch across and along your spine? Now inhale and slowly lift yourself up, stretching your elbows as far back as you can. Do you feel your chest stretching with all the air rushing into your lungs? Good. Repeat.

• Bellows pose: The aim of this technique is to breathe in as much air as possible. Think of your lungs like bellows. Place your arms by your side and forcefully blow out all your breath with a loud "whoosh." Now inhale as noisily as you exhaled. Keep this up and keep it noisy. How do you feel? Better?

The Reason We Don't Breathe Properly

It is a fact that the more oxygen you get, the better your brain, organs, and whole body in general function, and the more clear-headed you are. There are so many factors that inhibit proper breathing.

Do your clothes feel too tight? Vanity is probably keeping you from breathing healthily. Your entire life will change as soon as you begin to find joy in looser clothing and better fitting clothes.

How is your posture? Do you slump, like I used to, over the laptop? Some causes are more difficult to spot or alter. Are you dealing with a physical disorder? Are you experiencing side effects from a medication you're on? Do you have any food allergies? My breathing greatly improved when I noticed how creamy foods produced phlegm in my throat and reduced my breathing quality.

How to Breathe Through the Chakras

Chakras are energy points on your body through which energy flows. There are seven primary chakras you need to be aware of:

1. The crown chakra on top of your head.
2. The third eye chakra in the middle and slightly above your brows.
3. The throat chakra.
4. The heart chakra.
5. The solar plexus chakra.
6. The stomach chakra.
7. The chakra at the base of your spine.

Breathing techniques work to create a clear path through which air can move through your chakras to cleanse, feed, and fuel you. When the air travels through a clear path in your body, it is usually called an inner flute because it makes a sweet sound like a flute.

You can breathe through each chakra by focusing on the feelings at their locations. You can share the energy with your partner by having them inhale on your exhale while concentrating on their chakras. This back and forth fuels and empowers you both. The following exercises work wonders:

• Buddha breathing: Breathe in as deeply as possible onto your lower belly until it swells like a contented Buddha. This can be done alone or with your woman, facing each other or with your back to her back. This isn't a breathing technique that people jump at, because they don't feel very sexy with their bellies popping out. However, it is an excellent exercise to perform in the middle of sex. You can simply ask, "Do you want to do the Buddha breath?" If she agrees, come close enough for your chests and bellies to touch, then begin.

• Fire Breathing: This breathing technique gets you all fired up. All you need to do is take quick breaths in and out of your nostrils, making your belly pulsate rapidly. You can amp things up by raising and dropping your arms with each breath. This is an exercise to do by yourself, preparing to breathe with your partner for more intense connections.

• Synchronized Breathing: This exercise requires you to breathe in and out through your nostrils in sync with your partner. This will deeply connect you both and put you on the same wavelength. Simply sit cross-legged on a pillow or any comfortable surface while facing each other, ensuring your spine is straight. You should have a signal to begin. A wink is perfect. Few minutes into the synchronized breathing, close your eyes, and feel your energy patterns.

• Reciprocal Breathing: This technique requires you to exchange air with your partner. Think of it like you're breathing for each other. Get in the yab-yum position, and breathe in, while your partner breathes out, and vice versa.

• Golden Circle Breathing: Breathe in and picture the energy emanating from your sex center, rising through your body, past all your chakras to the top of your head. Then see it going back down to your sex center at the base of your spine before exhaling. As you breathe out, your partner breathes in and repeats the process.

- Bliss Breathing: Breathe in deeply through your nose, deep as you can. Exhale through your mouth, ignoring any sounds you might be making. Just smile.

3 THE PREPARATION

Before engaging in tantric activities, you need to be prepared for a magical ride. You're going to experience a delicious and satisfying rush of energy up and down your spine. This rush electrifies every cell from your head to your toes. The body becomes the bridge that connects the spiritual to the earthly on your road to fulfillment.

Think of yourself as a car, with your sex center as your gas tank. Your tires and chassis are the base center or first chakra, which keep you firmly on the road. Your breathing, combined with your sexual energy, serves as fuel moving through your gas line, which is your spine. Like every system in a car, your body's systems have to function for you to cruise effortlessly through life.

It isn't uncommon to find people who are not aware of the body temple that they live in. They take it for granted until they experience one breakdown or the other. Don't wait until you don't like what you see when you look in the mirror. These days, we abuse our bodies with a lack of sleep, overeating, toxic food, alcohol, and all sorts of terrible substances, which make us have regrets. We engage in a common form of abuse: Self-criticism. However, to participate in tantric sex, you and your partner must transform that hate into love.

How to Build Love for Your Body

An essential aspect of embracing the beauty and fullness of sex is observing your body, getting rid of negative attitudes, and replacing them with positive ones. I like to call these exercises "home play" because anything you engage in to increase pleasure should be fun and playful. You and your partner should practice home play separately because this is a very private and intimate moment you need to have with yourselves.

1. Get naked. Stand straight in front of a full-length mirror. Take a good look at all parts of yourself, beginning at your feet and slowly working your way up to your head. If you notice any self-criticism starting to bubble up, cut it short, and say something kind to yourself instead. Rather than, "My breasts are too little," you can say something like, "My breasts are perky and firm," Don't be concerned about lying; you are simply distracting yourself and being kind.

2. Inspect your genitals. As a woman, you can sit on any comfortable surface and use a hand mirror and flashlight to take a good look at yourself. Spread your lips and take note of the shapes, colors, and wetness.

3. Inspect your first chakra. This is also called the base center and is found around the anal area. It is a symbol of security. It can be easily observed if you squat with a mirror and flashlight. Look at the colors and observe the skin texture.

Now it is one thing to simply look and another to describe what you see. Men are faced with their genitals every day because it is so accessible, unlike a woman's. Women were trained not to take even a peek at what is down there, and today, some women not only shy but unsure. It is always a surprise when I'm faced with women, even the sophisticated ones, who have very little knowledge of their sexual parts. Tantric sex encourages full awareness of your genitalia, so you will describe your parts and compare them to the descriptions I will list below:
 • The sacrum is a triangular area found right above the tailbone, which awakens sexual energy when tapped.
 • The clit is much more than the knob, tip of bump that you feel. You may not know this, but it extends into the body through a shaft, which gives pleasure when stimulated.
 • The urethral opening is separate from the vaginal opening and lies in front of it.
 • A spongy tissue called the urethral sponge surrounds the urethra. It consists of ducts, blood vessels, and glands responsible for the production of fluids through the urethra when a woman is highly

aroused. These fluids are also called love juices or female ejaculate. They can be triggered by stimulating the G-spot located inside the vagina.

Now that you are both comfortable and familiar with your love parts, it is time to move on to other preparatory methods of tantric sex. This experience should be considered a tantric date. Having sex shouldn't merely be an act. It should be seen for what it is: A ritualistic experience that requires conscious actions and thoughts as a part of the seduction process. In tantric sex, every move you make serves multiple purposes: To get you in the mood, to relax your mind, to build suspense, to help you cherish your lover, and much more.

The preparation of yourself and the space for lovemaking requires you to pay attention to the tiniest details. This kind of care is a sign of reverence for each other and the time you spend together. It is an expression of the value you place on the relationship and yourselves. The tantric night of delight should start with making time for each other, a vital aspect some couples seem to ignore.

You Need to Make Time

There's simply not enough time. I have heard many complaints, but this tops the list. I can understand why it is a common complaint. Today's schedules are absolutely crazy, but that is also precisely why you need to pick a date for this rare kind of loving. You can begin with an hour or two hours at different times during the week. You both should pick a date and put it on the calendar. Sex might seem like a silly thing to put on the calendar. Still, it only affirms that your relationship is just as important as other things in your life, like your job, family relationships, and so on.

"But what about spontaneity?" You might ask. Not everyone would jump at the idea of organized sex because it doesn't seem like fun. However, when deciding to try your hand at a new exercise or self-improvement activity, you will be required to allot time and effort. It doesn't matter if it's weight lifting, meditative yoga or tantric sex. To ensure that your priorities stay in order, you need to schedule these activities, at least in the beginning. You can be spontaneous later.

Cleanup Consciously

You've been on dates, haven't you? So you've experienced playing dress-up, which involves cleaning up nicely to impress. If your relationship has seen a few years and now you tend to take each other for granted, tantric sex will take you back to the old days when you made significant efforts to please. Let's look at helpful guidelines for a conscious cleanup that can be done alone or with your lover:

1. Your fingernails should be clipped and clean. Trimmed nails are not only a turn-on but also hygienic, considering you'll be using them please your lover inside and out.

2. Ensure you brush your teeth, especially in preparation for a romantic activity with your lover. You don't want to whisper in her ear and have her struggling to breathe. Toothpaste with baking soda works wonders, then mouthwash for a fresh finish.

3. Take time to wash her hair while she does yours. If you have never done this before, it'll be even more meaningful.

4. Shave each other while making sure to be extra tender, so you don't bruise your skins. This activity builds a different kind of trust.

5. Give each other a pedicure. If she likes her toenails painted, paint them. Rub her feet.

6. Ensure that the lighting in the room or bathroom is perfect. Some bathrooms have either very low lighting or harsh lighting. Use rose-colored bulbs for your special evening or simply purchase a special lamp for the occasion. Candles are also beautiful, so decorate the floor and sink counters with scented candles.

7. Take a bath together with warm water.

8. Put some music on to set the mood. If you are feeling up to it, mount stereo speakers in your bathroom, or just play some tunes from your tablet or phone with a BlueTooth speaker.

9. Don't hold back on the scented soaps, soft brushes, bath mitts, and bath oils.

10. Place a mat at the bathroom door for when you both are ready to exit, so you don't step on the cold floor. In preparation for your exit, also get a soft bathrobe and plush towels.

The Bathing Ritual

We're all familiar with jumping into the bathroom for a quick swish in the bathtub or a quick shower after an exhausting day to prepare for sex. But when last did you just soak up in a bath with your partner? Deliberate and sensual bathing together is an integral part of tantric sex. The time spent in the tub is for more than merely washing up. It also helps to:

- Ensure you both enjoy the feeling of being in the water together.
- Make sure you both get to rediscover your bodies.
- Get your sexually fired up.
- Increase your awareness of one another.

The main point of this exercise is to transform something as simple as washing each other into a ritualistic practice done with conscious effort and attention. Instead of rushing over body parts with soap, take some time to linger on specific areas. Imagine you're giving each other a massage, but with soap. You get to slide and swish over your lover's skin as creatively as you would like. Make use of different kinds of touches to please your partner. Alternate between long, short, smooth, and circular strokes around areas like the butt and back. Trace your fingernails lightly on her skin, and slowly, gently dig into her flesh for intensity.

Like a massage, you should start with the nonsexual body parts to build anticipation before moving on to the sexual areas. Use your fingers to trace lines across and around her breasts and inside her thighs. Delicately wash her privates with an air of innocence, while intending to arouse her. It's called teasing. This can be a foreign experience for couples who are not used to doing these activities for one another, but it is very relaxing.

4 TANTRIC COMMUNICATION

An essential aspect of tantric sex is communication. There is a great deal of importance placed on the kind of communication between you and your partner. Some people tend to shy away from communication because it's just too intimate. Still, if you're here, you need to be prepared to communicate because that is what tantric sex is about, communicating verbally and physically to feel even more connected to your lover. Let's look at some key points to keep in mind while communicating:

● Eye contact. Maintaining eye contact during sexual activities is crucial. It means letting go of all your inhibitions and staring into her beautiful eyes. In tantra, it is a widespread belief that the left eye is the looking eye and the right eye, the receiving eye. You should look into your lover's right eye while communicating with her. Be sure to get into a position that will enable you to speak freely while maintaining eye contact. Another important thing is not to close your eyes as your lover speaks to you because you will need to observe the emotions expressed. You can't do that with your ears alone. They say the eyes are the windows to the soul, and they never lie.

● Remember to smile. Look interested in what your lover is saying. Don't look away or make uninterested facial expressions. Smile or simply sport a pleasant facial expression when you're communicating during sex. Tantric sex establishes a bond between you and your lover, so you're bound to smile anyways or, at least, look pleasant.

● Say what is on your mind. When engaging in tantric sex, I encourage you to think out loud. You aren't meant to hold back any thoughts or wait for the perfect opportunity. Tell your lover all that you are thinking. If you are enjoying something, say it. If you're not, communicate your displeasure. Speaking your kind will give your lover an insight to how you feel at every moment.

• Try to emote. Be present while communicating. Making gestures while you speak can help. Gestures help better communicate whatever you mean. Your facial expressions and hand gestures are just as important as your words, so don't be afraid to use them. Don't hold back your laugh, smile, or tears when speaking to your lover. If you can, avoid distracting behavior like grinding your teeth and cracking your knuckles. Simply gaze into your lover's eyes.

• Always encourage each other. When communicating with your lover, ensure that you support and give them room to speak as well. Communication has to be mutual, or it would be pointless. Say things that will require a response so that they get a chance to throw in a word or two. Provide your lover with ample time and opportunity to express her thoughts and feelings.

• Transparency. While communicating with your lover during or after sex, ensure that you make yourself clear. Nobody likes listening to a person who mumbles. It is crucial to know the things you want to say and how you intend to say it.

• Communication should be fluid. There should be flow to your speech, and flow between you two as well. You can't keep interrupting each other, or you'll be jolted right out of the mood. A tantric sex session can last for hours or as long as you two want it, so you need to be mentally and emotionally prepared to speak your mind. I don't mean talking too much because that will simply tire you out. I mean channel your feelings and thoughts properly. Let this energy course through you. That is the only way to truly let go.

• Truthfulness. Honesty is a crucial aspect of communication, so don't be afraid of your thoughts or speaking honestly. There's no room for lies or exaggeration in tantric sex. Keep it as true and as simple as it is.

5 TANTRIC SEX POSITIONS

The Sandwinder Position
This technique permits deep penetration and also allows for maximum eye contact. The bottom will lie with her side on the bed and raise the top leg to rest on the top's shoulder behind her. Now thrust as deeply as she would like, changing the speed and rhythm every now and then.

The Yam Yum Position
This is the ultimate tantric sex position. It is almost effortless to perform and permits enough body contact. The top will sit on a comfortable chair or bed with her back straight. The bottom will then straddle her lover and lock her legs around her back. Move slowly and build momentum.

The Padlock Position
This pose gives the top a good view of the beauty before her. The bottom gets on a high surface like the kitchen counter or table; then, she will lean backward onto her elbows to support her torso. The top gets in between her thighs and slides into her.

The Butterfly Position
The bottom gets on a high surface like a table and sits with her butt close to the edge. The top stands at the edge of the table facing her partner's butt and then raises both of the bottom's legs to rest on her shoulders. This will expose the vagina and tighten its canal because the legs are closed.

The Double-decker Position
Here, the top sits on the bed with her legs folded underneath her. The bottom faces away from her partner and positions her body right

above the strap-on. She positions each leg on either side of her partner's. Now she can lower herself onto her partner and move them both to ecstasy.

The Hot Seat Position

This position allows for both lovers to have equal control of the movements and actions. The top gets on the bed just like the previous position but with her legs spread this time. The bottom gets into the same position facing away from her partner and between her lover's open legs, with her legs closed. The top will slide in from behind while the bottom bounces herself up and down in front.

The Daily Grind Position

Friction from rubbing is very intense and intimate for both lovers. The bottom gets on her back while the top gets in between her legs and begins to grind her clit rhythmically against her partner's pubic bone or thigh. For extra friction, the bottom should grab her lover's butt and grind against her as well. This position is perfect for nipple biting, kissing, and eye contact.

Eve and Lilith

This tantric position sets the spotlight on Eve, who kneels on the bed, leans back to rest on her elbows, and wraps herself around Lilith seated on the bed facing her. This position allows Lilith to pleasure Eve to satisfaction by caressing her skin, breasts, clit, and much more. For extra funk, Lilith can slip her fingers inside Eve's mouth before or after massaging her insides.

Saturn's Rings (my favourite)

You and your lover should be seated on a comfortable surface with your legs bent and facing each other. Scoot forward until your groins are close to each other, and begin to pleasure each other with your fingers. To take things up several notches, make use of a double dildo to grind against, and simultaneously penetrate each other. A silicone double dildo is a perfect choice for this activity. Use as much lube as you would both like, and slide it in one after the other, using your hands to keep the toy steady. After a while, let go of the dildo and let your vaginas do the gripping. This way, your hands are free to caress each other.

The Girl Wrap Position

This is a modified version of the vanilla missionary position. The bottom lies with her back on the bed. She wraps her legs around her lover, who is positioned in between her legs. This allows her to thrust and be thrust into better.

It is important to note that no matter the position you go with, you should take advantage of every opportunity to connect with your partner. This means when it's a position that allows eye contact, lock eyes with her. Also, breathing consciously does wonders for the intense sensations you'll get during tantric sex. Even better, try breathing in sync. You could both inhale and exhale at the same time, or you could breathe in while she breathes out and vice versa.

6 TANTRIC MASSAGE

Tantric massage is a sensual and spiritual hands-on practice that is very different from regular massages. It acknowledges and makes use of energy, also known as the tantric essence of shakti. This massage can be used to foster the connection between lovers. It is not only sensual, but offers release physically, emotionally, and mentally.

It is common to think that a massage between lovers is all about reaching a climax, but that is a wrong assumption. Orgasms are a very possible and welcome by-product of this sacred practice; however, they are not the end goal. The ultimate goal is spiritual upliftment, relaxation, mental freedom, and a stronger connection between you and your lover. Let's look at the steps to achieve this:

1. Begin with her backside. You will need two tablespoons of any massage oil to get started. Rub the oil between your palms to warm them up a little before placing your hands on her lower back and sliding them upwards to her neck and shoulders, then downwards to her butt.

2. Hand slide movement. You have successfully coated her back only lightly with oil. Now, slide your fingers down her spine. Massage your way to her lower back, over her butt, and back up again. Slide your hands upwards to massage her neck, then work her shoulders thoroughly before working your way down her arms to her fingertips. Do this at least five times, and communicate while you do to keep in touch with what she likes and doesn't.

3. Kneading movements. Have you ever baked or seen someone bake? If yes, then you should have a pretty good mental picture of this technique. Here, you will squeeze her back and butt between

18

your other fingers and thumb in sinuous movements, squeezing with one hand then the other. Now move to a different part of her neck and repeat the movement. Do this until you have touched every area of her back and butt. Don't be worried about squeezing too hard. Her butt can take it.

4. The feather strokes. Before finally leaving the back and moving onto her thighs, apply feather-light strokes to her neck, shoulders, arms, back, and butt in this order. Keep it going for five minutes, and if you have long nails, lightly rake them across her flesh every now and then.

5. Foot caresses. For this, you will need to get more oil. Rub the oil between your palms until they feel warm. Drizzle a little more onto your partner's thighs, and work. Begin with the hand slide, then the kneading, working your way down her calf and up. After a few minutes, you can move to begin work on her feet. Drizzle a bit of oil onto each foot, and rub it in all the way up to her ankles. Knead downwards to her heel, soles, and toes. Slide your palms on the sole of her foot a few times. Rotate her ankle in both directions. Lastly, slide your finger in between her toes, gently pulling each toe away from her body.

6. Time to turn over. By now, your partner must be relaxed and very happy with your previous work. Help her turn over so that you can show her frontal area some love. Start with some oil on your palms, then a little on the body. Now begin to perform all the techniques above in order in that same order. When you are finished, simply allow her to enjoy how she feels. Don't expect a massage right then because they can be very relaxing. You can always get yours another day.

CONCLUSION

The privilege that comes with being human is our ability to generate euphoric energy in consciousness. This is what separates us from the animal kingdom. Even though there is much to learn through the observation of sex in the animal world, they clearly lack presence or consciousness. They do this based on instinct alone. Perhaps we have been influenced by this, as unfortunately for most, they hold on to dismissive behavior towards sex, seeing it as a purely instinctive activity, lacking spirit. This widespread notion has reduced sex to merely "bumping uglies" for the purpose of a climax. We live without ever experiencing the euphoric spiritual aspect of the magical, mystical act that sex really is.

Sex today is perceived superficially as an emotional or physical need. So, we pretend to be disinterested in it while our hearts remain confused. We know we have to "do it" every once in a while, but we make an effort to keep it in the dark. We are instantly gratified, and the physical need subsides, but deep down, we know something is missing.

Tantra doesn't seek confusion or indecision; it dispels all that darkness. It wants every part of you. It offers you excitement, movement, moments of stillness, orgasms, and much more, all wrapped in a beautiful package.

What do you get when you practice tantra? You get a complete and irreversible sex re-education. The increase in your sensitivity through tantra is a change that remains with you forever.

Tantra invites you to make love with consciousness, remaining aware through the act and after. All you need to begin is the intent to stay as present as possible. That's a good starting point. Where it leads or how it turns out does not matter; your ability to stay in the moment is everything.

Tantra isn't concerned about what you do but how you do it. There's no room for the superficial performance of sex for sex's sake. Tantra is more than that. It will open you and your partner's eyes to see the incredible oneness that you are.

Two souls, moving as one.

ABOUT THE AUTHOR

Florence Blue (born May 30, 1983) is an author and sex educator. She believes that we all are spiritual beings and sexual expression is essential in our life. She is very open-minded, tolerant and direct. Interested in sexual energy and integration of intimacy, body, mind and spirit. As a Coach Florence indicates connection between sex life, love and your partner.

Printed in Great Britain
by Amazon

25453521R00020